POCKET KANYE WI$DOM

WITTY QUOTES AND WISE WORDS FROM KANYE WEST

hardie grant books

MELBOURNE · LONDON

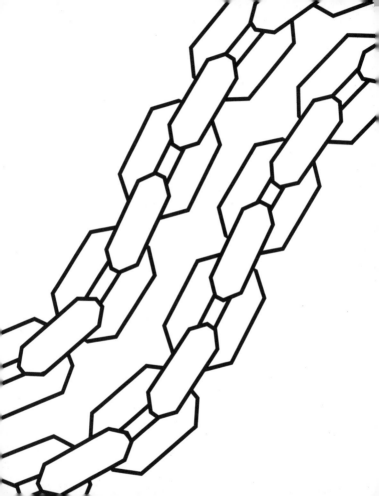

CONTENTS

KANYE WEST ON...

MONEY & SUCCESS

POCKET KANYE WISDOM

'For me, first of all, dopeness is what I like the most. Dopeness. People who want to make things as dope as possible, and, by default, make money from it.'

BBC Radio 1, Zane Lowe interview, September 2013

MONEY & SUCCESS

'I don't even listen to rap.
My apartment is too nice
to listen to rap in.'

BBC 1Xtra, DJ Semtex interview, November 2008

POCKET KANYE WISDOM

'I've gotta get my money
up to another level cause
it ain't on Jay Z level, it
ain't on Diddy level yet.'

Hot 97 Radio, featured in *The Hollywood Reporter*, November 27 2013

MONEY & SUCCESS

'I don't know if this is statistically right, but I'm assuming I have the most Grammys of anyone my age, but I haven't won one against a white person.'

The New York Times, 11 June 2013

POCKET KANYE WISDOM

'I think what Kanye West is going to mean is something similar to what Steve Jobs means. I am undoubtedly, you know, Steve of Internet, downtown, fashion, culture. Period.'

The New York Times, 11 June 2013

MONEY & SUCCESS

'I will be the leader of a company that ends up being worth billions of dollars, because I got the answers. I understand culture. I am the nucleus.'

The New York Times, 11 June 2013

POCKET KANYE WISDOM

'I am a black American male from Chicago… who had my rehearsal dinner at Versailles and then got married in Florence with a view of the entire city.'

GQ, July 2014

MONEY & SUCCESS

'… I believe money is important.
I think that artists have been
brainwashed to look at money
as a bad thing, and it's not.'

Papermag, 'Kanye West In His Own Words', April 2015

POCKET KANYE WISDOM

'You can't meditate me out of my ideas! You can't sedate me. What calms me down is success.'

Hot 97 Radio interview, featured in *The Hollywood Reporter*, 27 November 2013

MONEY & SUCCESS

'I'm talking about economic empowerment because the economics give you choices, the choices can help give you joy and freedom. And I'm trying to find that joy.'

Hot 97 Radio Interview, featured in *The Hollywood Reporter*, 27 November 2013

POCKET KANYE WISDOM

'I am in the lineage of Gil Scott-Heron, great activist-type artists. But I'm also in the linage of a Miles Davis, you know, that liked nice things too.'

The New York Times, 11 June 2013

MONEY & SUCCESS

'Just imagine if I woke up
one day and I was whack.
What would I do then?'

The Guardian, August 2005,

KANYE WEST ON...

MUSIC

POCKET KANYE WISDOM

'I am the number one human being in music. That means any person that's living or breathing is number two.'

The Wendy Williams Show, September 2007

MUSIC

'I am God's vessel. But my greatest pain in life is that I will never be able to see myself perform live.'

Storytellers, VH1, March 2009

POCKET KANYE WISDOM

'... I will go down as the voice of
this generation. Of this decade,
I will be the loudest voice.'

The AP, November 2008

MUSIC

'I definitely have OCD ... I have to be creative at all times and I have to learn. I don't know any other way. I'm a designer and rap is just one of my designs.'

The Observer, 12 August 2007

POCKET KANYE WISDOM

'I'm not going to sit here and defend shit. That shit is rock 'n' roll, man. That shit is rap music. I am a God. Now what?'

WMagazine, 19 June 2013

'I'll take opinions from anyone from Jay Z to a janitor, and I might value the janitor's opinion more.'

The Guardian, 5 August 2005

POCKET KANYE WISDOM

'I'm like, the anti-celebrity, and my music comes from a place of being anti.'

The New York Times, 11 June 2013

'I just dove more into rapping because I had a lot that I wanted to express, and I wasn't a really, really good singer.'

The New York Times, 11 June 2013

POCKET KANYE WISDOM

'There's nothing more to be said about music. I'm the fucking end-all, be-all of music. I know what I'm doing.'

Details, March 2009

MUSIC

[On the success of his album] 'You are in the presence of the champion. Bow in the presence of greatness.'

Wendy Williams Show, September 2007

POCKET KANYE WISDOM

'... We culture. Rap is the new rock and roll. We the rock stars.'

BBC Radio 1, Zane Lowe interview, September 2013

MUSIC

'Oh my God, I'm one of the greatest rappers in the world.'

Details, March 2009

KANYE WEST ON...
RELIGION
& ART

POCKET KANYE WISDOM

'The Bible had 20, 30, 40, 50 characters in it. You don't think that I would be one of the characters of today's modern Bible?'

BBC Radio 1, Tim Westwood interview, August 2007

RELIGION & ART

'I guess I'm religious because I really do believe that Jesus died for our sins.'

The Guardian, 5 August 2005

POCKET KANYE WISDOM

'I'm the closest that hip-hop is getting to God. In some situations I'm like a ghetto Pope.'

The Guardian, 5 August 2005

RELIGION & ART

'I'm like a vessel, and God has chosen me to be the voice and the connector.'

Storytellers, VH1, March 2009

POCKET KANYE WISDOM

'I am Warhol. I am the number one most impactful artist of our generation. I am Shakespeare in the flesh.'

SiriusXM Radio Interview, November 2013

RELIGION & ART

'I think I do myself a disservice by comparing myself to Steve Jobs and Walt Disney and human beings that we've seen before. It should be more like Willy Wonka…and welcome to my chocolate factory.'

SiriusXM Radio Interview, November 2013

POCKET KANYE WISDOM

'When I think of competition
it's like I try to create against
the past. I think about
Michael Angelo and Picasso,
you know, the Pyramids.'

Slate, August 2010

RELIGION & ART

'I am here to fight
for creativity.'

Grammy Awards, 2015

POCKET KANYE WISDOM

'Sometimes people write
novels and they just be so
wordy and so self-absorbed.
I am not a fan of books… I am
a proud non-reader of books.'

Reuters, May 2009

RELIGION & ART

'... I'm here to fight for the re-education of what celebrity is. To say, "Yes, we are celebrities, but yes, we're also innovators, we're also inventors, we're also thoughtful." '

GQ, July 2014

KANYE WEST ON...
HIMSELF

POCKET KANYE WISDOM

'Nobody can tell me where
I can or can't go.'

WMagazine, 19 June 2013

HIMSELF

'I'm doing pretty good as far as geniuses go ... I'm like a machine. I'm a robot. You cannot offend a robot.'

BBC Radio 1, Tim Westwood interview, August 2007

POCKET KANYE WISDOM

'I'm going down as a
legend, whether or not
you like me or not.'

BBC Radio 1, Tim Westwood interview, August 2007

HIMSELF

'I'm like a tree. I feed the branches of the people.'

The Daily Mirror, October 2010

POCKET KANYE WISDOM

'It's important to express my opinions… but I need to learn that sometimes it's not the right time to express yourself.'

The Observer, 12 August 2007

HIMSELF

'There's nothing I really wanted to do in life that I wasn't able to get good at. That's my skill.'

The Guardian, 5 August 2005

POCKET KANYE WISDOM

'Now, I just do exactly what
I want, whenever I want,
how the fuck I want.'

WMagazine, 19 June 2013

HIMSELF

'I care about everything.
Sometimes not giving a fuck
is caring the most.'

WMagazine, 19 June 2013

POCKET KANYE WISDOM

'… My ego is my drug. My drug is, "I'm better than all you other motherfuckers. Kiss my ass!"'

WMagazine, 19 June 2013

HIMSELF

'Come on now! How could you be
me and want to be someone else?'

The Guardian, 5 August 2005

POCKET KANYE WISDOM

'Because I talk so much
shit they give me over
credit just to shut me up!'

The Guardian, 5 August 2005

HIMSELF

'I am so credible and so influential and so relevant that I will change things.'

The New York Times, 11 June 2013

POCKET KANYE WISDOM

'My parents would say,
"Why are you such a ham?"
I was made to show off.
I was born to stunt.'

The Guardian, 5 August 2005

HIMSELF

'Maybe 90 per cent of the time it looks like I'm not having a good time.'

The New York Times, 11 June 2013

POCKET KANYE WISDOM

'Respect my trendsetting abilities. Once that happens, everyone wins.'

The New York Times, 11 June 2013

HIMSELF

'I understand culture. I am
the nucleus.'

The New York Times, 11 June 2013

POCKET KANYE WISDOM

[On his impulsive behaviour]
'Its only led me to complete awesomeness at all times. Its only led me to awesome truth and awesomeness. Beauty, truth, awesomeness.'

The New York Times, 11 June 2013

HIMSELF

'I don't care what your job is, you're not gonna talk down to me, you're not gonna try to get a rise out of me. I'm a man first.'

GQ, July 2014

KANYE WEST ON...

LOVE & LIFE

POCKET KANYE WISDOM

'I know people want to talk about the American Dream, but my dream is a world dream. It's a world in which everyones main goal would be to help each other.'

Papermag 'Kanye West In His Own Words', 2015

LOVE & LIFE

'I'm the type of soul that likes to be in love and likes to be able to focus. And that inspires me.'

The New York Times, 11 June 2013

POCKET KANYE WISDOM

'Any woman that you're in love with or that loves you is going to command a certain amount of, you know, energy.'

The New York Times, 11 June 2013

LOVE & LIFE

[On Kim Kardashian] 'I just see like, an amazing person that I'm in love with that I want to help.'

The New York Times, 11 June 2013

POCKET KANYE WISDOM

[On Kim Kardashian] 'She was in a powerful enough situation where she could love me without asking for money. Which is really hard for me to find.'

BBC Radio 1, Zane Lowe Interview, September 2013

LOVE & LIFE

'People have me pinned as a shark or a predator in some way, and in no way am I that. I wouldn't want to hurt anyone.'

GQ, July 2014

POCKET KANYE WISDOM

'… I feel like the type of girl I would be with is a fellow superhero. So we get that "already flying and now we're just flying together" thing.'

Details, March 2009

LOVE & LIFE

'People always tell you, "Be humble. Be humble." When was the last time someone told you to be amazing? Be great! Be great! Be awesome! Be awesome!'

The Atlantic, May 2012

POCKET KANYE WISDOM

[On Kim Kardashian] 'Our love story is like a love story for the ages.'

Hot 97 Radio, featured in *The Hollywood Reporter*, 27 November 2013

LOVE & LIFE

'I don't have one regret.'

The New York Times, 11 June 2013

77

KANYE WEST ON...

FASHION & STYLE

POCKET KANYE WISDOM

'I'm a pop enigma … I rock a bespoke suit and I go to Harold's for fried chicken. It's all these things at once, because, as a tastemaker, I find the best of everything.'

Spin, December 2007

'My goal isn't to "break through the fashion world", my goal is to make usable sculpture.'

Papermag 'Kanye West In His Own Words', April 2015

POCKET KANYE WISDOM

'I don't care about the thumbs-up or the thumbs-down. Fashion is something that's in my heart to do – in my spirit.'

Papermag 'Kanye West In His Own Words', April 2015

FASHION & STYLE

'There's no world that can stop me from what I love. Not the rap world, not the fashion world, not the real world.'

Papermag 'Kanye West In His Own Words', April 2015

POCKET KANYE WISDOM

'I'm going to be the first straight, hip-hop, loud celebrity, non-etiquette having, black out all the time, fresh-ass, super-tasteful designer of all time.'

SiriusXM Radio, November 2013

FASHION & STYLE

'Criticism can bother you, but you should be more bothered if there's no criticism. That means you're too safe.'

Hot 97 Radio Interview, featured in *The Hollywood Reporter*, 27 November 2013

POCKET KANYE WISDOM

'I had a style that was over-the-top, overly expressive, and it forced me to just lay back and be a little cooler.'

Details, March 2009

FASHION & STYLE

'It's funny to be so famous and noted for one thing, and to have so many people try to box you out of another form of art, even if you've proven you're an artist of one form.'

Papermag 'Kanye West In His Own Words', April 2015

POCKET KANYE WISDOM

'I paid my dues when I had to wear a kilt in Chicago, and friends would say, "What's your boy got on?" But there are warriors that have killed people in kilts in the past.'

Papermag 'Kanye West In His Own Words', April 2015

FASHION & STYLE

'I think the scariest thing about me is the fact that I just believe. I believe awesome is possible and I believe that beauty is important.'

Papermag 'Kanye West In His Own Words', April 2015

POCKET KANYE WISDOM

'When I entered the fashion
world, and I encountered a
lot of elitism and all that…
It just made me happy.'

TIME, April 2015

FASHION & STYLE

'I've put myself in a lot of places where a vain person wouldn't put themselves in. Like what's vanity about wearing a kilt?'

The New York Times, June 2013

POCKET KANYE WISDOM

'Fashion is something that's
in my heart to do – in
my spirit.'

Papermag 'Kanye West In His Own Words', April 2015

'I chose to paint sonically.
To chop samples in a
Warhol-type way.'

Papermag 'Kanye West In His Own Words', April 2015

POCKET KANYE WISDOM

'I'm going to be the
Tupac of clothing.'

SiriusXM Radio Interview, November 2013